PRAISE FOR *ON PURPOSE:*
HOW ENGAGEMENT DRIVES SUCCESS

Since 1986, Give Kids The World Village has brought more than 165,000 critically ill children and their families to Orlando for a weeklong visit at no charge to the family. How do they do it? It starts with purpose. Every person who serves at the Village, whether a paid staff member or one of hundreds of volunteers, is doing something that gives their life purpose and meaning. In her book **ON PURPOSE**, Pamela Landwirth, president and CEO of the Village, shows how this sense of purpose and meaning drives success—not only for individuals, but also for entire organizations. Using examples from the Village as well as several other companies, Pamela draws a blueprint of passion and purpose that every reader is invited to follow. Read this book to learn how one of the best run nonprofits in America is making a real difference—and how you can, too.

KEN BLANCHARD, *coauthor of* The New One Minute Manager® *and* Servant Leadership in Action

---

Succinct and inspirational, this book contains insight that is priceless to any business leader today. It emphasizes that, in retaining the brightest and the best people for your company, it is imperative to appeal to their innate thirst for purpose. It is essential to appeal to their hearts.

Like Pam Landwirth, it was my privilege to be part of the Disney team, leading people who found their true north in purpose—making their living by creating happiness and memories for families from around the world, and donating precious free hours to provide solace and respite for those in need. At Disney, Pam and I were surrounded by compassionate people who knew, firsthand, that life has a meaning that extends well beyond making a living. To go to the next step—to make a life—involves opening your heart to others: something that tens of thousands of Disney cast members have done over the years at Give Kids The World Village.

Pam Landwirth has a capacity for emotional outreach that is boundless. I have long believed that a leader is a person with a head for business and a heart for people, and Pam has achieved that wonderful balance. This book pays forward her wisdom.

It is with gratitude to Pam and Give Kids The World, and what both have meant to me, that I am thrilled to highly recommend this book to you.

MEG GILBERT CROFTON, *President (Retired), Walt Disney Parks & Resorts Operations—United States & France*

I have worked with Pam Landwirth for nearly 14 years. She is one of the most positive, energetic, dedicated and faithful leaders I have ever known. Make-A-Wish and Give Kids The World have had a special partnership for decades as we have entrusted tens of thousands of wish children and their families to GKTW for their wish.

Their attention to detail for every single wish child who comes to their Village is truly remarkable and I am convinced it is because it starts at the top. Pam has set the tone for GKTW to be a magical place, free of worry for these special children and their families.

In this book, Pam has brilliantly captured the essence of living a fulfilling life. The various stories you will read will touch you deeply because they capture people at their best – when they Give/Serve/Share, as the Village puts it.

And the news is even better for corporations because Pam demonstrates that giving, serving and sharing is not only good for people, it is good for companies! There is so much emphasis these days on improving employee engagement, culture and teamwork. Pam outlines practical ways to accomplish all the above while making a huge impact on our world.

After reading this book, I know you will be inspired to give, serve and share more. And in that process, you will make this world a better place and you will become a better, happier and more fulfilled person.

DAVID WILLIAMS, *President & CEO Make-A-Wish America*

With this book, Pam Landwirth has provided a perfect model for how any individual or organization can bring purpose into their life. It has been reported that 80 percent of people in the workforce are not engaged and don't like their job. Add purpose to the job, and you and your teams will excel. Every Cast Member at Disney understands that we all have different roles in the show, but we have only one purpose and that is to, "make sure every single guest has the most fabulous time of their life." GKTW is fueled by purpose. Add that same fuel on purpose to your organization and watch it soar.

LEE COCKERELL, *Executive Vice President (retired and inspired), Walt Disney World® Resort and best-selling author of* Creating Magic, The Customer Rules, Time Management Magic *and* Career Magic

ON PURPOSE

HOW **ENGAGEMENT**

DRIVES **SUCCESS**

Pamela Landwirth

Printed in the United States of America.
Library of Congress Control Number: 2018967223
ISBN: 978-1-949639-57-5

Cover Design: Melanie Cloth and John Carrillo

For my dad

Anyone who has spent much time around me knows that there has not been a more significant influence on my life than my late father, Dr. Warren "Marty" Martinson. He taught me about service and leadership. By example, he showed me the value of living life with child-like wonder.

I have traveled the world. I have met and worked with many remarkable individuals from whom I have gleaned a wealth of valuable insights that I draw upon every day. However, I have never seen such a collection of positive traits embodied in any one person as there were in my father. Kindness. Intelligence. Humor. Compassion. Conviction. Fortitude. Determination. Humility. And countless other qualities that made him a unique influence in not only my life, but in the lives of many others who were blessed to know him.

This book, and the message it offers, is for him.

TABLE OF CONTENTS

ACKNOWLEDGMENTS

Throughout the process of writing this book, I've had the encouragement and collaboration of friends, colleagues, and advisors. They've all made valuable contributions, and this book simply would not exist without their collective gifts of talent, time, and commitment.

Before I recognize them, I also want to thank the one person who, other than my dad, is most responsible for where I am today – Henri Landwirth. Henri brought me to the Village and showed me how hope and purpose bring light to even the darkest days. Hope truly is the most precious gift you can give another human being.

I am profoundly grateful to both my dad and Henri, just as I am to those who helped make this manuscript a reality:

To Kathleen Tagle, thank you for being my tireless cheerleader, advocate, and yes, taskmaster. Without your continuous urging and encouragement, this book would be an unfulfilled dream.

To Mattea Kramer and Jim Stratton, thank you for distilling the message and for helping me weave my thoughts and anecdotes into the fabric of the overall narrative.

To Chad Hostetler, thank you for your contributions to the development and organization of the message and for generating focus.

To John Carrillo, thank you for lending your unparalleled creativity to the design and layout.

To all those who were so generous with their time in interviews, thank you for sharing your insights and reflections on the importance of engagement.

To all of the incredible leaders I worked with at Walt Disney World, thank you for helping me find my gifts.

To Henri, thank you for creating a place that allows me to give them away.

To all the staff and volunteers at Give Kids The World Village, thank you for exemplifying engagement each and every day.

To my children, Matt, Katie, and Victoria, thank you for sharing Gramps' passion for service.

To all of the precious children who have visited the Village and those yet to come, thank you for being my inspiration.

"MY LIFE WAS INCOMPLETE"

As president and CEO of Davidson Hotels & Resorts, John Belden runs a company with thousands of employees, hundreds of millions of dollars in annual revenue, and a footprint stretching from Hawaii to Florida. This is why it's more than a little surprising that his life could be transformed by a plush polar bear suit.

Let me explain.

John is a board member of Give Kids The World Village, a nonprofit "storybook" resort in Central Florida that I've been fortunate enough to lead for twenty-five years. For more than three decades, Give Kids The World has been providing weeklong, cost-free dream vacations to critically ill children and their families.

Not long ago, John flew from his company's headquarters in Atlanta to Orlando to be part of a strategy session I'd scheduled for our corporate partners.

The meetings took place over two days, and I'd taken care to arrange volunteer opportunities for those participating in the sessions. Day one was a Thursday, which happened to be the day Give Kids The World staged its weekly Winter Wonderland celebration for visiting children and families.

John's assignment for the party was to serve as the happy, dancing polar bear. Never mind that it was ninety degrees outside. Never mind that John runs a major hotel-management company that includes some of the most prestigious brands in the business. He cheerfully stepped into the hot, furry costume and headed outside to perform in the Winter Wonderland parade.

During the parade, a little girl spotted the polar bear and instantly fell in love. When John approached her and her family, she popped up to give him a hug. In that moment, the girl and the polar bear became fast friends.

Every night at the Village, we offer tuck-ins from a six-foot rabbit named "Mayor Clayton"—our organization's official mascot—and his bunny bride, "Ms. Merry." They make the rounds, tucking visiting children into bed and saying good night. On this particular night, the little girl from the parade had a special request: could her polar bear friend, she asked, tuck her in instead of Mayor Clayton?

The polar bear immediately agreed.

So, when the party was over, he joined the girl and her family and headed back to their villa. There, he held her hand, gave her a hug, and gently tucked this sick little girl into bed. She quickly drifted off to sleep.

At the strategy meeting the next morning, I asked everyone about their volunteer experience from the night before. John spoke first, rising from his chair.

"I have a beautiful family," he said. "And I run a very successful business. I have wonderful friends in my life. But I will tell you, my life was incomplete until my volunteer experience last night."

Silence filled the conference room as the weight of John's words settled on the group. John had an enviable personal and professional life. He was nothing if not successful. But he felt something had been missing until he brought happiness to a child facing her own mortality.

John was articulating the power of purpose—the impact of what it's like to make a difference in the lives of others. He was stunned at how much his small gesture—a simple tuck-in—had meant to a child in need. That, in turn, had filled him with a renewed sense of purpose. It was a powerful moment, one that lit a fire in John and affected him in a deeply personal way.

When people devote themselves to charitable causes, they often have an experience like John's. They discover a new sense of passion and energy, and a deeper sense of purpose in their own lives. They feel inspired and important because they see how they fit into a larger picture of improving the world around them.

Unfortunately, many of us live our lives without that sense of purpose. We may be successful; we may even be happy. But there's often something missing—there's a hollow place in our lives—and it leaves us feeling vaguely unfulfilled.

This problem is particularly acute in the workplace. Today, far too many workers don't see a deeper meaning in their daily vocation.

Their work is too often just a means to a paycheck, not a higher calling.

The situation is undeniably costly—costly for individuals, who go through the motions without passion or purpose, and costly for employers, who are paying workers simply looking to punch a time clock.

This book is my modest effort to push back against that tide of apathy. It's about purpose and meaning and supporting causes that matter. It's about businesses and organizations that understand that employees and customers want—and *need*—life to be about more than pay stubs and products.

In the pages that follow, I'll introduce you to a range of sterling companies—like Davidson Hotels & Resorts—that have recognized how important it is to inspire passion and purpose among their team members. The leaders of these corporations realize they must "do good" while doing well if they are to attract and retain the talented workforce that allows them to turn impressive profits.

More often than not, these companies have done so by forging meaningful partnerships with worthy charities, including Give Kids The World Village.

I've been honored to serve as president and CEO of the Village since 1995. At the Village, we're all about purpose, and we nurture that deep sense of meaning in our employees, our donors, a small army of volunteers, and a dedicated collection of corporate partners. These corporate partners have aligned themselves with our organization to be part of a larger social mission—to offer their employees a connection to a cause that transcends their daily job responsibilities.

The notions of purpose and service have been part of my life since childhood. When I was growing up, my father led the Volunteers of America chapter in Lexington, Kentucky—a nonprofit organization dedicated to helping the most vulnerable and underserved individuals. I was expected to be there every weekend, working in the thrift store next to my mom and dad in service to a greater mission. Implicit and explicit in this expectation was the idea that we're put on earth to help others.

My dad had been the president of an electrical supply company when I was very young, but when he was in his early forties, he pursued—and achieved—a long-held dream of becoming a minister. He became one of the first Presbyterian ministers ordained to serve people addicted to alcohol or drugs, and our house was soon filled with people coming to him for counseling. He did that work in addition to running the Volunteers of America chapter and serving as a pastor in Somerset, Kentucky.

His lessons of service lived in my DNA, and by the time I graduated college, I thought my path was clear. I'd apply to law school, get my law degree, and then work with people who needed help navigating the legal system. But first, I'd spend a summer doing what a lot of other recent graduates were doing: working at Walt Disney World.

I soon discovered I loved helping guests at Disney and that my efforts and skills were truly valued there. I had no idea that this was the beginning of a career that would span nearly two decades.

It was an exciting time to be at Disney, and the company offered me a range of opportunities. I spent time in Casting, Human Resources Development, and Resort Operations; helped open Euro Disney; and had a role in developing the Disney Approach to People Management, and Disney's Approach to Quality Service.

These amazing opportunities kept me energized and excited about going to work. In fact, my days at Disney were so rewarding, it was hard to imagine working anywhere else.

Until, in 1992, I met a man named Henri Landwirth.

Henri was a Holocaust survivor who had come to the United States after World War II with just twenty dollars to his name. He eventually moved to Florida and worked his way up in the hospitality industry, becoming the owner of several hotels.

Since Henri owned a Holiday Inn near Disney, nonprofit, wish-granting organizations often asked him to provide free accommodations to critically ill children visiting Central Florida on their "wish trip." Henri always said yes.

It was a modest operation until Henri learned about a wish child named Amy. She'd been scheduled to stay at Henri's hotel, but her other travel arrangements had taken too long to finalize. Amy was very sick, and she simply ran out of time.

When Henri learned what had happened, a new sense of purpose roared to life. He vowed that logistics would never again prevent a sick child's wish from being fulfilled. So, at the age of sixty, when most people who reach his level of success look forward to retirement, Henri created a process—and later, a place—capable of making those wishes happen within twenty-four hours, if necessary. The place—Give Kids The World Village—opened in 1989. Today, the Village has grown to nearly one hundred acres and has served more than 165,000 children and families from around the world.

Each family that comes to us receives a weeklong vacation complete with accommodations, meals, entertainment, theme park tickets, and much more. No child is ever turned away, and there is never any charge.

I became involved with the Village in 1992—drawn by Henri's passion for his mission—and I've been here ever since. It's an extraordinary place that, despite the medical issues of our guests, bubbles with joy, hope, and, above all, purpose.

Families arriving at the Village might think they've stepped into a dream world, or a world designed by children. There's a magical castle and an enchanted carousel. There's an ice cream parlor that opens for breakfast and a miniature golf course. There are villas that escaped from the pages of a storybook and fire hydrants painted as imaginary characters. There is color and energy and laughter everywhere.

But the most distinctive features of the Village are the faces of the children.

These are kids battling some of the most serious illnesses known to medicine. Their lives and the lives of their families have been overwhelmed by hospital visits, medical procedures, and worry—constant worry. But you'll never see that at the Village.

Instead, you'll see a little girl in a wheelchair beaming like a sunflower. She's been to Disney and met a princess. She's ridden on a Village train and felt the breeze on her face. She's had ice cream for breakfast, danced with a star fairy, and—for the first time ever—splashed in a pool.

She's had a magical week—the best in her life—because the mission of Give Kids The World has ignited a sense of purpose in people from across the globe. At the Village, volunteers fill 1,800 shifts a week. That's 93,600 volunteer shifts a year. Supporters come—absent any financial reward—to dedicate their time, talents, and passion because it adds purpose to their lives.

Likewise, corporations big and small partner with us because they recognize that doing *good* ultimately helps them to do *well*. They have chosen to pursue purpose, and in so doing, they have unlocked profit.

It is clear to me that purpose and meaning drive success. It's a not-so-secret formula that every company and organization should make part of their culture. In the chapters that follow, I'll show you how.

PART ONE

MAKE IT PERSONAL

There's a quote about living with purpose that says it all. Who said it first it isn't clear, but it's often attributed to the legendary college football coach and master motivator Lou Holtz. Holtz, a member of the College Football Hall of Fame, is one of the most positive people on the planet, not to mention a really funny guy. Here's what Coach Holtz says about living a meaningful, happy life: "We all need four things in life: something to do, someone to love, something to hope for, and something to believe in."

You might not think this has a whole lot to do with managerial science—but it does, and management experts are increasingly tuning into the deeper issues of purpose and meaning as keys to motivating employees. Increasingly, employees and customers are looking for companies whose goals, values, and commitment to a purpose align more closely with their own.

Most employees and most employers want to do more than make and sell widgets, even if they produce the best widgets in the business.

They want to make a difference. They want to take pride in their company's commitment to corporate social responsibility (CSR), to its role in making the world around them better. Doing so connects them at a deeper level to their workplace—something that's not happening at far too many companies today.

Consider, for instance, that a Gallup survey of 230,000 employees in 142 countries found that only 13 percent of the workforce was "engaged" in their work.[1] For the vast majority of employees, work is what a Harvard Business School professor and a psychologist jointly described in *Harvard Business Review* as "a means to an end, where people suffer through their jobs in hopes of finding time for those things that matter more: family, faith, hobbies, vacations, even watching TV."[2]

Think about how sad that is. Suffering through work just to reach the end of the day—only to collapse on the couch to watch TV? That is a far cry from having a sense of purpose, from finding those four things Coach Holtz says lead to a meaningful, satisfying life.

---

1   Ante Glavas, "Corporate Social Responsibility and Employee Engagement: Enabling Employees to Employ More of Their Whole Selves at Work," *Frontiers in Psychology*, 7:796, May 31, 2016, https://www.ncbi.nlm.nih.gov/pmc/articles/PMC4886691/.

2   Teresa Amabile and Steve Kramer, "To Give Your Employees Meaning, Start with Mission," *The Harvard Business Review*, December 19, 2012, https://hbr.org/2012/12/to-give-your-employees-meaning.

Employees who are suffering through work surely aren't engaged, and the cost of that disconnect is steep. Employee engagement affects everything from the corporate culture to the bottom line. An employee who's disengaged—who's going through the motions—demands more supervision and, invariably, does second-rate work.

It's hard to put a dollar figure on that, but the other associated cost is easier to calculate. Estimates suggest that employee turnover—the toxic, but predictable, fallout of disengagement—costs anywhere from a few thousand dollars per employee to nine months' wages (or more) for a salaried worker.

That's what we're facing in a world where only four in ten employees even know what their company stands for, or how its brand is distinct from that of competitors, which is how Chris Groscurth described our state of affairs in the *Gallup Business Journal*.[3] Employees need to understand and embrace the goals, purpose, and values of an organization. Then, and only then, will they really care about their work and their company.

Now here's the really good news: you don't need to be running a children's charity or other nonprofit to nurture a sense of purpose. Even if there's no obvious social cause behind what your business does every day, you can still create an environment in which employees feel that they're part of something bigger than themselves.

In this chapter, you'll read about three exceptional companies, ranging from small to multinational, that have taken that wisdom and turned their workplaces into environments where employees feel a personal sense of meaning in what they do every day. Then we'll talk about how that translates into better results for the company

---

3   Chris Groscurth, "Why Your Company Must Be Mission Driven," *Gallup Business Journal*, March 6, 2014, http://news.gallup.com/businessjournal/167633/why-company-mission-driven.aspx.

while they're making a positive difference at the same time.

How Davidson Hotels Makes it Personal

You might not be familiar with Davidson Hotels & Resorts, the company led by John Belden—the CEO and Village polar bear I introduced you to earlier. But you surely know the heavy hitters that hire Davidson to manage their hotels. The list includes Hyatt, Hilton, Sheraton, and Marriott.

The leaders of Davidson pride themselves on an impressive and unusual claim: they say their employees receive the same care and compassion that hotel guests receive as paying customers. If that sounds unlikely, consider that Davidson, which is based in Atlanta, received a 2018 Top Workplaces award from the Atlanta Journal-Constitution, a designation given out on the basis of employee feedback.

Davidson is no mom-and-pop operation, either. It has seven thousand team members who are collectively responsible for 13,600 hotel rooms. How has Davidson succeeded at building and sustaining such a positive company culture over such a large organization? The answer sounds hopelessly hokey, but it's actually enormously profound.

"It's simply one word: love," John told me. "We love what we do, we love who we work with, and we love our mission. And it's not just about the work we do, but also the way we do the work."

Davidson has been around for forty-four years, meaning virtually no one on the current team was present for the company's founding. And yet the corporate culture is imbued with a sense of history and responsibility in which team members of today see themselves as stewards of the company and its culture for the next generation.

And for Davidson, an integral part of that culture is being a part of Give Kids The World. For twenty-eight years, the company has been a steadfast partner to the Village. John calls the partnership a "huge" part of who they are. Every year, Davidson sends a couple dozen team members to the Village—and those team members experience firsthand the magic of being at the Village, of seeing children giggle and laugh, even as they fight critical illnesses. John says that the time they spend volunteering "lights a flame in them."

"Seeing the engagement that the wish families have with the volunteers and the staff of the Village," John says, "the unbridled joy of a child who, for maybe the first time in their lives, has had some semblance of normalcy or hope—that experience never leaves you."

When they've finished volunteering, and they've rejoined their teams at Davidson hotels across the country, employees don't forget about community service. Instead, they host do-it-yourself fundraisers that raise a whopping $300,000 every year for Give Kids The World. One year, two Davidson team members rode a Tom Sawyer-style raft down the Mississippi River to raise money—and, in the process, unleashed an infectious sense of enthusiasm and generosity throughout the company.

As Davidson team members devote themselves to supporting Give Kids The World, John is certain that the company gets back just as much as it gives. He says Davidson's commitment to Give Kids The World sends a message of purpose to all team members.

"They see a company that cares passionately about doing good," he told me. "They feel a sense of pride at being a part of a business that's about more than just running a business." He emphasizes that Davidson has one of the lowest turnover rates in the hotel industry. "You can never pin it on one thing, but Give Kids The World is a part of that success."

The culture of doing good guides Davidson's corporate strategy, too. John has been quoted in hospitality trade journals as saying there's a right way to do business and a wrong way to do business. It's easy to "cut corners" and "do business the wrong way in an effort to generate money," he said. But that's not how Davidson operates.

Consequently, Davidson has chosen not to cut costs or fire staff to boost short-term earnings. Nor does it embrace charitable endeavors just because it's trendy. John's predecessor oversaw the initial partnership between Davidson and Give Kids The World. And when John took over twelve years ago, everyone knew the alliance would endure—because it's part of the company's very fabric.

"When I retire," he said, "there will be no doubt that Give Kids The World will remain part of our DNA."

Walmart Lets Employees Identify Worthy Causes

With more than seven thousand employees and thirteen thousand rooms under management, Davidson leaves a pretty big footprint. But it pales in comparison to Walmart. With more than two million employees, Walmart is the world's largest retailer. That's why it was an especially big deal when internal surveys revealed that the company suffered from a lack of employee engagement. To address the problem, company leaders developed an innovative platform for employees called My Sustainability Plan. The strategy was designed to bring corporate social responsibility—and, along with it, a sense of individual purpose—to every employee, from top executives to store managers to the frontline crews stocking shelves.

Connecting hundreds of thousands of Walmart employees in 9,600 stores across twenty-eight countries, the My Sustainability Plan platform gave employees the chance to decide where and how they wanted to have an impact on the world around them. The platform allowed employees *themselves* to identify worthy causes. Then it actually tracked and showed their impact.[4]

Ultimately, more than 500,000 Walmart employees chose to participate in CSR initiatives through My Sustainability Plan. Let that sink in for a moment: more than half-a-million people—essentially the population of Atlanta—chose to be part of the plan. As a result, they produced a staggering thirty-five thousand new ideas that benefitted both the company and the environment[5]—and the environment was only one of the causes Walmart employees opted to support.

Researchers have found that the presence of a social mission at work helps employees feel a sense of meaning in their lives; it helps them feel good about themselves. And when their work provides that deeper sense of fulfillment, they don't just feel happier; they feel a stronger sense of self that helps them identify in a deeper way with their work and employer.

The school of thought known as "engagement theory" even holds that employees who feel a sense of congruence between their own values and their employers' values believe that they can be more authentic at work. In the words of Dr. Ante Glavas, a professor at the University of Vermont's Grossman School of Business, employees who feel that there's a consistency between their values and their

---

4   Carol Cone, "Stop Engaging — Start Fulfilling: A New Era of Employee Engagement," *Sustainable Brands*, May 8, 2017, http://www.sustainablebrands.com/news_and_views/organizational_change/carol_cone/stop_engaging_%E2%80%93_start_fulfilling_new_era_employee_en.

5   Ante Glavas, "Corporate Social Responsibility and Employee Engagement: Enabling Employees to Employ More of Their Whole Selves at Work," *Frontiers in Psychology*, 7:796, May 31, 2016, https://www.ncbi.nlm.nih.gov/pmc/articles/PMC4886691/.

company's values can "bring their whole selves to work."[6] As a result, the hours they spend on the job are no longer divorced from what they actually value; work has become something they can look forward to in its own right.

When people feel this sense of meaning at work, they feel engaged. When they're engaged, they feel a sense of ownership over their work. And when they feel a sense of ownership over their work, they're more passionate, productive, and innovative. They also become effective—and profitable—agents of the companies they represent.

All of this effectiveness and profitability is rooted in the simplest concept of all: contributing to the greater good.

Mears Transportation: You Should Be Able to Reach Out and Touch it

That idea may seem self-evident, but it works only when it's embraced by an organization's leaders—leaders like the Mears family of Orlando's Mears Transportation. Since its founding in 1939, Mears Transportation has recognized the importance of creating a company culture that nurtures a sense of purpose.

Paul Mears Sr. began the company with just three taxicabs and a simple idea: provide great customer service all the time. In the decades that followed, Mears turned those three taxis into more than six hundred. Guided by the vision of his son, Paul Mears Jr., the company expanded into shuttle vans, motor coaches, and luxury vehicles. Today, some three thousand people earn their living working

---

6   Ante Glavas, "Corporate Social Responsibility and Employee Engagement: Enabling Employees to Employ More of Their Whole Selves at Work," *Frontiers in Psychology*, 7:796, May 31, 2016, https://www.ncbi.nlm.nih.gov/pmc/articles/PMC4886691/.

for Mears Transportation. Many of these employees are deeply loyal to Mears Transportation—in part because the company has given them more than just a job.

Mears Transportation was one of a handful of companies that served as founding partners to Give Kids The World. Henri Landwirth got to know Paul Sr. because the company was always dropping guests off at his hotel. The two men became friends, and Henri—who was never shy about asking for help—contacted Paul Sr. as he was planning to launch Give Kids The World. He wondered if Mears could provide transportation for visiting wish families.

Paul agreed on the spot, and then made an astonishing commitment: Mears Transportation would provide free transport from the airport to the Village (or, in the earliest days, to Henri's hotel), to and from the theme parks, and back to the airport for any wish families that wanted it. Henri was stunned by the magnitude of the gift, and he considered Mears's support to be a crucial contribution to making Give Kids The World a reality.

Paul Sr. didn't commit to helping Give Kids The World in order to better his business; he did it because he felt it was the right thing to do. But what his enterprise gained in return was something that money can't buy: employees who find purpose and meaning in what they do for a living.

The company's current president, Paul Mears III, hears it all the time. One driver told him he considers it "an honor to be part of these once-in-a-lifetime [wish] trips." Another said he never tires of "pulling through the Disney World gates and seeing tears of joy running down the faces of an entire family. You can tell that some of these families have fought hard just to have that moment."

Over the course of its partnership with Give Kids The World Village, Mears Transportation has done much more than provide rides. Its top executives have made a conscious effort to share the Village's story with everyone in the company ranks, including new members of the team, who come to see the cause as their own. Give Kids The World has now been a priority for three generations of Mears Transportation's leadership and drivers, all of whom share a sense of purpose in serving children with critical illnesses. Every time a driver provides transportation to a wish family, they feel that their work is meaningful. They know they're making a difference, and they can see and feel the results in a very immediate way.

Researchers have found that mission-oriented activities are most likely to boost employee engagement when they're a tactile part of employees' job description, as opposed to something on the periphery, or a mere line in a company newsletter.[7] There are plenty of wonderful organizations and charities across the country that are doing great work, but if the employees of a corporate partner are unable to visualize—or, better yet, *feel*—the impact of the charity they're supporting, then such a partnership is unlikely to provide a real boost in employee engagement. In contrast, when purpose-driven work becomes part of a company's basic activities, it is most likely to have a transformative effect on engagement. When employees can feel the impact of their work, it's personal.

Make it Personal, Literally

A partnership with Give Kids The World has helped countless businesses foster a sense of purpose among employees. Likewise, at the Village, we strive to "make it personal" by serving every wish child in a unique way. Here's a window into this work that has ignited such a

---

7   Ante Glavas, "Corporate Social Responsibility and Employee Engagement: Enabling Employees to Employ More of Their Whole Selves at Work," *Frontiers in Psychology*, 7:796, May 31, 2016, https://www.ncbi.nlm.nih.gov/pmc/articles/PMC4886691/.

sense of purpose in so many of our corporate partners:

At seventeen, Micah was older than many of the kids who come to the Village. And unlike many of our guests, Micah showed no outward signs of his illness.

Because his illness wasn't obvious, he looked like he should be able to do everything his peers could do. But he couldn't, so he always felt like an outsider.

When Micah's illness eventually made him eligible for a wish, he wanted to visit the Florida theme parks, but he wanted something else, too—something simple and heartbreaking: he wanted to feel important.

At school, for so long, he'd felt simply invisible. He hated that feeling. What he wanted, even for a moment, was to feel like he mattered—to be treated like royalty.

At the Village, we knew what we had to do: we would make him king for a day.

We created and wrote a script for a crowning ceremony. We prepared the throne in the Village's Castle of Miracles. We found a crown and assembled a royal court.

When Micah arrived at the Village, he was led to the Castle and greeted by his royal "subjects." He was crowned king by a knight and dressed in royal garb. Then we held a "pirates and princesses" party with King Micah presiding over the affair.

"Seeing my son being crowned was very touching and special because of the joy he was experiencing," Micah's mom said.

Micah wore his crown throughout his entire week at the Village. He moved with a newfound happiness and confidence. His mom later said that this new self-assurance stayed with him after he went home and returned to school. It seemed that we had achieved the impossible.

Now, here's what you need to understand: in the early years of Give Kids The World, we wouldn't have created a customized experience for Micah—what we now call a "personalization." We didn't offer personalizations because they're logistically difficult, and they gobble up staff and volunteer resources.

But about a decade ago, little by little, the scales began to shift. We began looking at the information we receive from wish-granting organizations on all our wish kids, and we realized it was a treasure trove. These organizations told us each child's favorite food, candy, activity, superhero, prince or princess, color, and so on. The information was a terrific window into the minds of our visiting kids.

We began using that information to make custom wish bags for every child coming to the Village, and our entertainment team used it to create a program of parties—one for every night of the week—based on what our kids are clamoring for. We also realized we could mine those preferences to create one-of-a-kind experiences for children who made small, personal requests as part of their larger wish. Micah wanted to visit the theme parks, but he also wanted to feel important.

Likewise, a little girl named Anna wished to visit Disney World, but she also wanted to feel like a princess and dance with her father. So while Anna was on her wish trip, we made arrangements for Disney World's Princess Belle to come by the Village. In our Castle of Miracles, Princess Belle helped Anna choose a gown and gave her a princess makeover. Then, when we turned on the music, Anna's dad lifted her from her wheelchair and they danced.

Anna's and Micah's experiences have made it abundantly clear that customized wishes must be part of what we do. Yes, they can be challenging, and we often need to be incredibly quick on our feet, but we've found that they can be so deeply meaningful that we simply can't *not* do them.

Purpose must be personal.

Whether you're a massive company like Walmart, a big company like Davidson Hotels & Resorts, a family business like Mears Transportation (or a nonprofit like Give Kids The World), effective leaders must find ways for people to find personal meaning and satisfaction in their organizations.

Your employees, your customers, your supporters: they all need purpose in their lives. Businesses and organizations that understand this will outpace the competition.

How to Make it Personal

- Follow the remarkable model set by Davidson Hotels & Resorts, and make it a company policy to treat your employees with the same care and compassion that your customers receive.

- Everyone needs four things in life: something to believe in, something to do, someone to love, and something to look forward to. Give your employees something to believe in by making mission-oriented service a part of their job description.

- When purpose-driven work becomes part of a company's core activities, it is most likely to have a transformative impact on morale and productivity. When employees can *see* and *feel* the impact of their work, it's personal.

PART TWO:

FORGE PARTNERSHIPS FOR THE COMMON GOOD

The wisdom of offering a sense of purpose to employees in order to boost engagement isn't limited to employees. Research shows that embracing a social mission is just as important to your customers.

"CSR is a powerful differentiator at the register, as 90 percent of global consumers would switch brands to one that is associated with a good cause, given similar price or quality,"[8] reports Sustainable Brands, an industry association serving brands committed to sustainability. Nine out of ten consumers around the globe are motivated to patronize brands that have a social mission. The most successful companies and organizations build connections to their customers in ways that go far beyond satisfaction with a product or service, by appealing to their desire to make a difference.

Indeed, consumers are becoming more wedded to the idea that the companies they patronize should be making our world a better place. The trend cuts across generations. Some 85 percent of all US consumers say they would switch brands to one with a social mission. A staggering 91 percent of millennials say they would do so.[9]

It's also no secret that many historically successful corporations are struggling to win over millennial customers, which represents a significant business dilemma. As *Business Insider* has pointed out, the eighteen-to-thirty-four-year-old set is now reaching its prime spending years.[10] Baby boomers are retiring at a rate of around ten thousand a day—but there are seventy-five million millennials in the US who are only gaining greater purchasing power.

"[Millennials] want companies to be actively invested in the betterment of society and the solution of social problems," reports *Forbes*.[11] And as Mashable has noted, citing research by Cone Com-

---

8   Sustainable Brands, "Study: 81% of Consumers Say They Will Make Personal Sacrifices to Address Social, Environmental Issues," March 27, 2015, http://www.sustainablebrands.com/news_and_views/stakeholder_trends_insights/sustainable_brands/study_81_consumers_say_they_will_make_.

9   Cone Communications, "2015 Cone Communications Millennial CSR Study," Key Findings, http://www.conecomm.com/research-blog/2015-cone-communications-millennial-csr-study#download-research.

10 Daniel Mahler, "An Emerging Retail Trend Is Key for Attracting Millennials," *Business Insider*, October 27, 2015, http://www.businessinsider.com/how-important-is-sustainability-to-millennials-2015-10.

11 Sarah Landrum, "Millennials Driving Brands to Practice Socially Responsible Marketing," *Forbes*, March 17, 2017. https://www.forbes.com/sites/sarahland-

munications, "If your brand doesn't support social causes, it's missing out on a huge audience."[12]

Who can afford to overlook the millennial demographic—or the group that follows them, "Generation Z"? Silly question—the answer is no one. Nor do you have to.

The solution to the dilemma of how to win over millennials represents a win for shareholders, customers, employees, and the global community of which we are all a part. It's time for companies offering every type of good and service to make social impact part of what they do.

"It's no longer a question if consumers care about social impact," reports Nielsen from a global survey on corporate social responsibility. "Consumers do care and show they do through their actions. Now the focus is on determining how your brand can effectively create shared value by marrying the appropriate social cause and consumer segments."[13]

That might sound like a tricky undertaking. It's one thing to say that every organization should pair its products or services with a social mission, but it's another thing to figure out *how* to do that—and how to do it in a way that enhances, rather than hurts, the bottom line. Can you make more money *and* have a positive social impact? The answer is yes—as long as you're working with the right recipe. In this chapter, you'll read about how companies, including

rum/2017/03/17/millennials-driving-brands-to-practice-socially-responsible-marketing/#6c15ac2c4990.

12   Matt Petronzio, "90% of Americans More Likely to Trust Brands That Back Social Causes," *Mashable*, January 11, 2015, https://mashable.com/2015/01/11/corporate-social-causes/#vuNFbPBRzPqk.

13   Nielsen, "Global Consumers Are Willing to Put Their Money Where Their Heart Is When It Comes to Goods and Services from Companies Committed to Social Responsibility," Nielsen Global Survey on Corporate Social Responsibility, http://www.nielsen.com/us/en/press-room/2014/global-consumers-are-willing-to-put-their-money-where-their-heart-is.html.

Procter & Gamble and Wyndham Hotels & Resorts, have achieved out-of-the-ballpark results in terms of both profitability and charitability—by forging the right partnerships.

Procter & Gamble Makes a U-Turn

In 1992, a Procter & Gamble brand manager named Dina Howell came to Give Kids The World Village with an overnight bag and a simple, if unpleasant, assignment. She'd been instructed to head down to the Village and terminate a relationship.

P&G had been supporting the Village for about three years at that point, but the arrangement—a coupon program that generated more than $100,000 in charitable donations annually—wasn't delivering the expected sales from retailers. Company leaders wanted to eliminate the program, so they dispatched Dina to deliver the news.

"I was told to go down and fire them," she says. "So I got on a plane, and off I went."

You should know that Dina Howell is tough. A P&G executive for more than twenty years, and former CEO of one of the world's most influential shopper marketing agencies, she has broken off plenty of deals that weren't working out. She figured she'd show up at the Village, meet with Henri, and give him P&G's message: "It's time to go our separate ways."

But Henri had other plans. Instead of heading into his office, Henri insisted on giving Dina, who'd never been to the Village, a tour. As they walked the property, Henri described the mission of Give Kids The World.

He told her that this is a place where some of the sickest children in the world come to reclaim time stolen by illness. At the Village, there are no hospital visits or medical procedures, no days packed with doctor appointments or consultations. For one amazing week, Henri explained, these kids and their families can just laugh, play, and be together.

As he walked Dina through the Village, Henri stopped parents and asked them about their experience. The endorsements tumbled out. They said their time at the Village was healing and happy and stress-free. It was the best time of their lives. It gave them hope, strength, and a sense of peace. Dina, eyes welling up behind her sunglasses, was overwhelmed.

"You'd have to have a stone heart not to see and feel what was going on there," she told me recently. "For me, it was looking into the eyes of the mothers. You could just see what this place meant to them."

At that point, she said, "I knew I couldn't do what I'd been sent to do."

So she laid out a plan with Henri. She'd return to Procter & Gamble headquarters in Cincinnati and argue the Village's case. She'd revise the coupon program to make it work better for the company and its retail partners. And she'd stress to her bosses that it was in the company's interest to keep supporting the Village—to be part of that "greater good."

In presenting the Village's case to P&G, Dina pointed out that employee engagement improves when workers feel their company is focused on more than just the bottom line. People want to work somewhere that cares about them and the larger world—somewhere that does well by doing good—and she argued that P&G's connection to the Village helped the company to retain and recruit talent.

Her pitch worked. P&G stuck with the Village, and Dina became one of our biggest champions. She provided the resources to reshoot photos for all our public-relations materials, introduced us to several retail partners, and created a plan to fund the House of Hearts, the building where visiting families are welcomed to the Village. Over the years, Procter & Gamble has donated more than $16 million in support of our mission.

Dina has been a part of Give Kids The World for more than twenty-five years; she currently serves on our board. She calls her relationship with the Village "the most meaningful thing I've done in my professional life."

She also firmly believes that companies can improve their bottom line by joining forces with a mission-driven organization.

"I've found it's very motivating for employees to work for companies that do great things for others," she says. "Give Kids The World does great things for sick kids, and employees want to support that."

Fortunately for us, the Village offers a particularly poignant opportunity for P&G—and other corporations—relative to other charities. Because the Village is a happy, lively resort that visitors can see, touch, and experience, it's easy to show employees their impact.

"It's not conceptual, not just an idea," Dina says. "You can go the Village and immediately see the benefit of what they do."

Extreme Village Makeover: Lessons from Wyndham

Leaders who make social impact a company priority can spur employees to accomplish incredible, even ridiculous, things. In the case of Orlando-based Wyndham Vacation Ownership, the team joined forces to do something amazing—something everyone thought was impossible—and, in the process, generated national publicity that reached millions of viewers.

Wyndham, a member of Wyndham Worldwide, is the largest vacation ownership company in the world, with fifteen thousand employees. For years, it has made volunteerism an integral part of its company culture, giving an eight-hour "wish day" to every employee. That's a fully paid day on which employees can volunteer at any charity they choose. It was Wyndham's longstanding track record of community service that led Give Kids The World to turn to Wyndham when it came time to renovate hundreds of villas here at the Village. What happened next was all thanks to Wyndham's leadership—and, more specifically, to Gary Rall.

Gary was a vice president at Wyndham when his boss, a friend of mine, asked him to see how Wyndham could become involved with the Village. At that time, we were finishing renovations on forty of our 140 villas, and we still needed to update the rest. But it had taken us almost a year to do the first forty, and we were looking for suggestions on how to speed up the work. We'd calculated it would take about thirty months to renovate another one hundred villas, and that would hurt our ability to host wish families.

Gary had never heard of Give Kids The World, and he already had a plate full of projects for other charities. Nevertheless, he dutifully came out to the Village to check things out. Almost instantly, the former college football player was hit hard by the magic of the Village.

"I was absolutely blown away," he said later. "Many things stood out to me, but one particular thing really touched me. It was a family of five. The child who was ill was in a wheelchair, had tubes connected to a tank of oxygen, and didn't have any hair. What she did have was the biggest, brightest smile on her face."

Gary immediately became one of our champions.

One night over dinner with his family, Gary began talking about the Village, and about how we had one hundred villas in need of renovation. He said that we'd completed forty in ten months and he worried it would take us years to finish the job.

"By the time they get to the end," he said, "it's almost going to be time to start renovating the ones they finished in the very beginning."

Just then, Gary's son, Zach, a middle-schooler, piped up.

"Dad, how many units do you renovate (for Wyndham) every year?"

"About five thousand, plus or minus," Gary replied.

"Well, they only have a hundred. Couldn't you do those in a week?"

Gary laughed. "*Dude*, you can't do *that* many in a week!"

But the crazy idea was now planted in his head, and the more he thought about it, the less impossible it seemed. He was confident the job couldn't be done in just one week ... but maybe in *two*. So Gary began to strategize in the same way that he approached his commercial projects.

"In a typical renovation cycle, we're doing hundreds and hundreds [of vacation rentals] at a resort," he explained later. "Most of the contractors do ten, twenty, forty in a week or two weeks, depending on the scope and the scale."

So, Gary began to think about the Village renovation as ten contractors each doing ten units. And with that mental shift, his son's logistically outrageous concept of "Extreme Village Makeover" became a reality.

It would take four thousand gallons of paint, three thousand electrical outlets, and one hundred thousand square feet of flooring material. It would also take tremendous commitment and an incredible amount of heart from the people on the Wyndham team. Gary set the tone, throwing himself completely into the project. By then, he believed deeply in the mission of the Village. He also saw the project as a valuable team-building opportunity for his company.

His enthusiasm for the effort was contagious. It prompted hundreds of associates from Wyndham to show up and volunteer. And it wasn't just their eight hours of company-paid "wish day" time that they volunteered, either. They used their own time off. Some came on weekends; others came at night after work. For two weeks, Wyndham—and a huge team of contractors—was all hands on deck, twenty-four hours a day. Literally. Gary spent the entire two weeks living at the Village with many of our Give Kids The World team members.

"They put their own blood, sweat, and tears into the project," said Gary of his teammates. "I was overwhelmed by it. To see everybody roll up their sleeves and do that was just amazing."

He was also amazed by the fact that his team was undeterred by bad weather.

"We did the project in January," he recalled recently. "When I originally approached some of the contractors—a lot of them are from the north: northern Illinois and Ohio and Rhode Island and New Jersey—they were actually pretty excited about leaving the cold and coming down to Florida in January to do this project. Lo and behold, that January had some of the coldest days we've had in a long time. When I watched our employees suffer through the cold, doing physical work, it was a sight to be seen. They were all bundled up—and it didn't stop them."

During the project, Gary discovered many Wyndham employees were already volunteers at the Village, while others had family members who'd come on their wish trips. Now, for droves of Wyndham employees, the shared experience of tackling Extreme Village Makeover supercharged morale. Together, they completed all one hundred villas forty-six minutes before the two weeks were up.

"It created a tremendous amount of camaraderie with the team," Gary told me. "During Extreme Village Makeover, I saw departments that don't normally work together working side by side. I saw our legal team out there when the weather was in the low forties. I saw them with hats and scarves and gloves on, cleaning the playground—washing and wiping down every piece of equipment in frigid temperatures."

The entire nation got to see the same thing when ABC turned Extreme Village Makeover into a national story on *Good Morning America*. In that moment, Wyndham became a name that millions of people connected with a good cause and the excitement of doing something miraculous to promote the common good. A wish child named Alyssa described the impact of her time at the Village to *GMA*'s millions of viewers, and we explained how Wyndham had made the project possible without compromising our ability to serve children like Alyssa as the result of a prolonged renovation period. Wyndham truly had made a difference.

Since those miraculous two weeks in January 2014, Wyndham's support for the Village has been unwavering. Gary emphasized that Wyndham has been made better in the long term by being a partner to Give Kids The World. The positive publicity created a ripple effect for the company, not only in the way that customers view Wyndham, but also in how team members relate to one another.

"There's a lot of negativity going on in the world today," he told me recently. "There's a lot of controversy on a lot of different subjects and topics. Everyone put that aside to do this project. They worked together on one cause, and it brought them closer together. It just really brought this true sense of community."

In the years since, many of the contractors who worked on the Extreme Village Makeover have continued to volunteer their time at the Village, as well as at other charities in their own communities. The experience at the Village was so meaningful for them that it prompted greater volunteerism.

"These guys were personally touched," Gary told me, "and they're all paying it forward."

This would never have happened if the Wyndham leadership had rejected the idea of serving the common good *and* their bottom line. When they looked for a formula that would allow them to do both, they hit a home run.

"We Move Your Life"

For leaders of one of the nation's top moving companies, the inspiration to forge a bold partnership for the common good came from an eleven-year-old boy from California who was battling leukemia.

Keaton came to Give Kids The World in August of 2002, and after his visit, he began speaking to support groups about how his wish trip had lifted his spirits. He wrote to me saying his time at the Village had reminded him of how much he mattered to the people in his life. His real wish, he said, was for people to care about him because he was a person, not because he was a sick kid. I still have that letter.

Around the same time, Wheaton World Wide Moving, one of our corporate partners, held its national conference in Indianapolis. They asked if a wish child might like to address the group. We thought immediately of Keaton, who happily agreed.

As suspected, Keaton was a natural. On the stage, he looked out across the hundreds of conference attendees and delivered a singular message.

"Don't pity me," he said. "Take your wish to help people and put it to a good cause. I'd like it if that cause was Give Kids The World because it's changed my life and my family's life. But don't pity me. It's not about me. It's about you doing something for this cause."

Even while battling leukemia, Keaton's focus was on helping other kids.

The next morning, Keaton ate with some of our staff, wolfing down steak and eggs and everything else in sight. He hadn't eaten that much in months, his dad later told me, because of the chemotherapy.

The Wheaton folks were similarly energized by Keaton's memorable speech, and their leadership asked Keaton if he'd appear at next year's conference, too. Keaton was unsure what he'd say in a second speech, but he told them he'd be there.

That was in October. In November, just after Thanksgiving, Keaton went in for surgery because the cancer had spread to his lungs. He never fully awoke from the surgery, then slipped into a coma, and passed away before Christmas.

In honor of Keaton's personal mission to help other kids, Wheaton made a momentous decision to become a permanent sponsor of the Village. That's how we came to build "Keaton's Korral," underwritten by Wheaton. Twice a week, the Korral transforms part of the Village into a trail-riding adventure, where wish kids—even those who use wheelchairs—can ride a horse or pony. More than simply a thrilling activity for our kids, horseback riding has valuable therapeutic effects.

After making this remarkable commitment to the Village, Wheaton adopted a new company motto: "We move your life." They saw themselves as not merely moving customers' belongings from one location to another, but also helping people to move forward in their lives. The alliance with Give Kids The World, Wheaton's leadership realized, was a perfect fit.

Soon, word started to get out about the company's exceptional charitable commitment, and Wheaton became a newsworthy company.

"We've gotten excellent publicity from newspapers and magazines about the good that we do," Wheaton chairman Stephen Burns told me, noting that it has given them a valuable boost in a crowded marketplace. "It helps distinguish us from our competition," he explained. The company has seen customer referral rates improve as a result of their now decades-long partnership with the Village because, as Stephen points out, people simply like doing business with companies that think beyond the bottom line.

Even as Wheaton benefited from greater publicity, the partnership was also a boon for Wheaton internally. It's hard to overstate the impact Keaton had on the Wheaton employees who heard him speak. His story has become legendary, familiar even to those employees who came along years later. Stephen has watched as his employees have become ad hoc spokespeople for the Village. They've dreamed up fundraising ideas, like sponsored events and golf tournaments. Wheaton drivers have gotten involved, too, stopping by the Village to visit when their routes bring them through Central Florida.

Stephen often hears directly from his employees how meaningful the relationship with Give Kids The World has become. One person told him that her past employers had encouraged their employees to give to charity, but it had always seemed peripheral to their work. At Wheaton, Give Kids The World is part of the mission and fits seamlessly with the theme of the company's core business.

I regularly attend Wheaton's annual conferences to tell employees about the impact of their support. As I talk about the children they've helped, I watch people wipe away tears. Afterward, I'm always overwhelmed as the employees tell me again and again how much the relationship means to them.

"When you pull your team together for a cause that has nothing to do with making money, it seems to join them in a bond that is deeper and more lasting," Stephen has told me. He calls it a "cementing effect" and believes it has helped reduce turnover.

Today, Wheaton prominently displays its philosophy on the company website:

> *Wheaton isn't just a moving company—we're a team of people, caring individuals concerned about the welfare of future generations. Because of that, we feel compelled to help make our communities healthy and vibrant, as well as environmentally sustainable. To that end, we take an active role in our community.*

Anyone can post a feel-good message online. But at Wheaton, the words carry weight. They represent who the company is and what it does—day after day, year after year.

When You Stick to Your Values, Wonderful Things Happen

Several years ago, Give Kids The World had a great opportunity to partner with American Airlines. In a hugely generous move, the airline wanted to put $500,000 toward building us a new facility. The initial meeting with company representatives went well, as Henri and I discussed with them the idea of renovating our pool area to include an amphitheater and a splash garden. Everything was clicking into place, but as the meeting wound down, we ran into some unexpected turbulence.

"And we just want to see a sign that says, 'This was made possible by the employees of American Airlines,'" said then-marketing director Bob Stoltz. "That's it."

Henri's response was polite but immediate.

"We can't do that," he said. "You'll notice there are no signs for any of our corporate sponsors here."

It was a policy that dated to the Village's founding. Henri didn't want corporate logos and signs splashed everywhere. He worried it would dim the magical glow of the resort. The Village was a place to escape, not be bombarded by ads.

We were deeply grateful for corporate support, but we weren't interested in advertising for companies inside the gates of the Village.

The team from American Airlines was surprised by his reaction. A little back-and-forth ensued; at one point, Bob suggested calling the new facility "The Park of DreAAms."

"That's not going to fool anybody," Henri said.

Both of us had begun to realize that we probably weren't going to be getting this gift after all. I felt the disappointment creeping over me.

Finally, Bob asked, point blank, "You're going to turn us down because of principles?"

"Yes," we said.

"If we do this for you, it opens the floodgates for everyone," Henri added. "Every corporate sponsor would turn around and possibly pull their support unless their name was on a sign."

And that ended the meeting. The American Airlines marketing team went back to their Texas headquarters and relayed the whole story to Bob Crandall, then the company's CEO.

We figured the deal had fallen through. I was saddened that our wish kids wouldn't get a new amphitheater and splash garden, but I knew we had made the right decision by sticking to our values and not being swayed by a dollar sign.

Then something unexpected happened at American Airlines headquarters. Bob Crandall was stunned to learn we'd turned the company down, but he was impressed by our stand.

"I like an organization that stands by its principles," he told his team. "Make it $1 million, and we don't need anything."

Eleven months later, the new Park of Dreams (not "DreAAms") was virtually complete. The project had become so important to American Airlines that it sent a platoon of employees to help with the finishing touches and the ribbon cutting. Volunteering had helped to create a sense of ownership in the effort.

At the Park of Dreams dedication, I noticed that one of the "finishing touches" was a whirligig topped by a small airplane bearing the letters "AA" on its tail. I turned to Bob Crandall—who gave me a Cheshire cat grin, knowing that it would come down the next day.

American Airlines employees continue to support the Village to this day through the Something mAAgic Foundation.

The Practical Magic of Volunteerism

At Give Kids The World, there are 1,800 volunteer shifts *every week*. We believe that makes us the largest permanent site for volunteerism in the world. Getting so many people to commit a significant share of their lives without any compensation is possible because they know they're contributing to something larger than themselves. It has also led to extraordinary stories of volunteerism—and extraordinary partnerships.

With different people coming to the Village for every possible type of volunteer service every week of the year, it's a huge undertaking to manage and motivate that army of volunteers. Yet we have found a way to motivate them, even absent any financial payoff.

Indeed, we're able to keep our volunteers engaged and motivated because "we offer such a tangible environment," says Caroline Schumacher, our VP of operations, who started as a volunteer at the Village when she was in college. "Our volunteers are critical to what we do. And our volunteers *want* to staff it because they can see and touch that mission right then and there. And those kids are going to smile at them and those parents are going to make eye contact with them, whether it's a moment in which they're serving waffles or a moment in which they're checking them into their villa. Or it's somebody just being patient with them, and slowing down and listening."

Our volunteers get to provide that. They get to bring families surprise and delight, something that's often in short supply when those families return home. Their weeklong vacation is an escape, and our volunteers, carried along by the tide of *purpose*, escape right along with them.

For some people, like Joe Koch and Brad Loewen, it becomes all-consuming.

Joe was a Philadelphia postal worker for thirty-eight years, dedicated to the motto that "neither snow nor rain nor heat nor gloom of night stays these couriers from the swift completion of their appointed rounds." But when Joe retired to Central Florida in 1994, he found his true purpose at Give Kids The World.

In retirement, Joe would get up before dawn so he could be at the Village by 5:30 a.m. Often, Joe would volunteer six days a week. For more than two decades, Joe dedicated himself to the Village and its families, finding purpose in the face of one tragedy after another.

During his time as a volunteer, Joe lost his wife and his son. He battled prostate cancer and survived quadruple bypass surgery. Even when Joe began to experience the early stages of Parkinson's disease, he kept coming to the Village, buoyed by the good feeling he found in helping others.

In the time Joe spent with us, he put in more than twenty thousand volunteer hours—the equivalent of working forty hours a week for over ten years. Only recently, as Joe's health faltered at the age of eighty-nine, did he stop coming to his beloved Village.

"Life is tough," Joe said in an interview with the *Orlando Sentinel*. "But if you have something to get up for in the morning, and you have a chance to help people, don't worry about tomorrow."

Brad Loewen took a very different path to the Village.

His first contact came after his son, who had a rare genetic disorder, was granted a wish trip to the Village. Initially, Brad was skeptical. In the first three years of Noah's life, Brad and his wife, Nicole, spent more than six hundred days in a hospital. Brad wasn't eager to spend Noah's wish trip surrounded by more illness.

"I did a little research," he told me later, "and I started warming up to it. You stay in homes, not a hotel. They take good care of you. There are parties for the kids every night. You can have ice cream all day long. But only when we went there and experienced how all the illness and negativity disappears when you're on that property, did I really get it. It's all about joy and peace and hope—not just for wish kids, but also for their parents, their siblings, and their caregivers."

Brad and Nicole developed such a connection to the Village that in 2012, several years after the passing of their son Noah, they moved from their home in Winnipeg, Canada, to Central Florida so they could volunteer regularly at Give Kids The World. Brad even expanded his paramedic- and firefighter-training business, opening a school in the US so the family could be eligible to stay here permanently.

Brad's company is now the largest private fire academy in the world, training six hundred to eight hundred students each year. He's turned over daily operations of the business to his senior management team so he can spend more time volunteering at the Village. Brad's employees know all about his family's experience—a Give Kids The World flag hangs in the entryway of each of his schools—and supporting the Village is part of the company's mission.

Brad told me his employees "have that passion each and every day they come to work, knowing they're supporting the greater good. They know the *why* behind our business and the reason we run it like we do."

Forge Partnerships for the Common Good

- Consumers want the products and services they purchase to support a social mission. It is possible to serve the common good *and* the bottom line; companies must determine how to align their brand with the right social cause.

- Companies such as Procter & Gamble, Wyndham Vacation Ownership, Wheaton World Wide Moving, and American Airlines have found creative ways to forge partnerships to deliver priceless social impact while boosting their reputation with customers.

- By serving a social mission, these companies didn't just generate valuable publicity; they also saw significant internal benefits as their teams became passionate about the charitable mission and felt greater loyalty and enthusiasm for their employer.

PART THREE:

CONNECT THE DOTS

Blake Mycoskie founded TOMS after a trip to Argentina, where he learned that many Argentinian children lacked shoes. TOMS is now a highly successful for-profit enterprise, operating with a "One for One" strategy in which the company donates a pair of shoes for every pair sold. The company draws a direct line between selling its products and helping people in need. It has also generated more than $400 million in earnings to date.[14]

---

14 Brian Rashid, "Why More and More Companies Are Doing Social Good," *Forbes*, April 25, 2017, https://www.forbes.com/sites/brianrashid/2017/04/25/ why-more-and-more-companies-are-doing-social-good/#7cb7afe2db07.

Mycoskie did something important when he crafted the TOMS business model: He connected the dots across the landscape of customer needs and wants. He married a laudable social mission with a simple, stylized product. He also told the story of the connection between product and purpose in a way that was easy for customers to understand and support.

Of course, most companies weren't explicitly founded with a social mission like that of TOMS, but that doesn't mean they can't connect the dots between their company and key trends across the consumer landscape. And it doesn't mean they can't tell a compelling story for their customers, employees, and all stakeholders.

In this chapter, you'll read about two well-known corporations—Hasbro and the Alex and Ani jewelry company—that have connected the dots in meaningful ways. Their products are captivating to customers, in part because they're much bigger than the products themselves.

Alex and Ani: Much More Than Jewelry

Alex and Ani isn't struggling in the earnings department. According to *Forbes*, the jewelry maker's revenue went from $5 million in 2010 to more than *$500* million in 2016.[15] Last year, the company's founder, Carolyn Rafaelian, appeared on the cover of *Forbes* under the headline "The Richest Self-Made Women."

It's an understatement to say that Alex and Ani, which Rafaelian founded in 2004 and is now worth an estimated $1.5 billion, has offered customers precisely what they want, precisely when they've

---

15   Clare O'Connor, "Bangle Billionaire: How Alex and Ani Founder Carolyn Rafaelian Built an American Jewelry Empire," *Forbes*, May 17, 2017, https://www.forbes.com/sites/clareoconnor/2017/05/17/carolyn-rafaelian-alex-and-ani-richest-self-made-women-billionaire/#715aa2ea3f11.

wanted it. The company's incredible growth came as the jewelry market was moving away from anonymous baubles and toward accessories that carry a particular message, purpose, statement, or even energy. From the very beginning of the company, Alex and Ani jewelry was always intended to radiate positive energy. And in the years since its founding, the company has also developed jewelry that carries specific messages linked to charitable goals.

In 2011, the company created a line called Charity By Design, which devotes a portion of all jewelry sales to designated nonprofits. To develop the products in this line, Alex and Ani has collaborated with more than fifty charities, including UNICEF, Big Brothers Big Sisters of America, Toys for Tots, and Give Kids The World.

A wish-granting organization called A Wish Come True first introduced Alex and Ani to Give Kids The World. From the beginning, we were astonished at the depth of their commitment to us as a charitable partner.

Representatives of Alex and Ani flew from Rhode Island to Florida to visit the Village. The plan was for their designers to come up with a custom charm bracelet that would raise money for our work, and they put a tremendous amount of time and thought into finding just the right symbol for the charm. What they ultimately proposed was a "sweet treats" ice cream cone charm, symbolizing our on-site ice cream parlor.

In July of 2014, our first Charity by Design bracelet launched. Over the next two and a half years, that single design raised enough money to fund ninety trips for wish children and their families.

But that was just the beginning of Alex and Ani's support for Give Kids The World. In 2016, the company created a holiday-exclusive charm to benefit our work—and that one raised around a quarter of a million dollars. Meanwhile, after the "sweet treats" charm had been on the market for a couple of years, the company said it was time to come up with another design on our behalf. Sales typically decline for any design after about two years.

And so, in April of 2017, Alex and Ani introduced an entirely new charm to benefit Give Kids The World: this time, a fairy. But even the company's series of charms doesn't represent all of its efforts on our behalf.

Staff from local Alex and Ani stores volunteer at the Village four times a year. When the "sweet treats" charm was still on the market, they often scooped ice cream for wish kids at the Ice Cream Palace. Now that we've done a fairy charm, they volunteer in the Castle of Miracles, where a magical star fairy places a gold star, personalized by each wish child, on the ceiling or walls.

Company volunteers also help our gift fairies deliver presents to visiting children. And the company hosts fundraising events in its stores around the country; "Charmed by Charity," they call it. This gives us the opportunity to engage directly with the company's customers. During these fundraisers, the store donates a portion of sales from *all* charms—not just our custom charms—to Give Kids The World.

Alex and Ani's impressive financials speak for themselves; customers are wild for the products. The company doesn't simply offer attractive jewelry, nor does it simply offer beautiful jewelry at affordable prices. It offers jewelry that carries a deeper meaning. Customers feel good about wearing every Alex and Ani design. The product isn't merely a beautiful object; it's a *feeling*.

This is the very embodiment of how the jewelry market has changed over the past decade. Alex and Ani connected the dots from what customers wanted and what the company could provide—and they have done so in a way that tells a story that's much larger than a bracelet.

That connection has been meaningful for employees and customers alike. At Give Kids The World, we've had the chance to hear directly from Alex and Ani team members about what it means to them that their job responsibilities include supporting the Village. Here are some of the things they've told us:

"We are so in love with what you all do."

"What you all are able to do is truly inspiring and we are so blessed to be entering into a partnership with you."

"The Village is magical! Looking forward to what is yet to come!"

When a team is so energized by their work's underlying mission, they can't help but pass that enthusiasm along to customers. The company has now donated more than $50 million to its nonprofit partners across the globe, including more than $500,000 to Give Kids The World. Alex and Ani employees have logged over 8,800 hours of volunteer service—the equivalent of more than four *years* of service for a full-time employee.

By connecting the dots, Alex and Ani has created a business model in which customers rave about the products in part because of the social mission, and in which employees are enthusiastic and loyal to their employer because they feel a deeper sense of purpose. It drives them to serve customers better, which, in turn, generates warm feelings for the company. It is a powerfully virtuous cycle.

The Groundbreaking Philanthropy of Hasbro

The toy giant Hasbro has been riding that cycle for years. It's worked diligently to develop an extensive CSR portfolio—one that would earn the company the number one ranking on *Corporate Responsibil-*

ity Magazine's prestigious "100 Best Corporate Citizens" list in 2017.

Our relationship with Hasbro began, surprisingly enough, with a cold call and a little white lie.

It was 2005, and you could say I was connecting a few dots of my own. I'd gotten it into my head that the Village needed its own version of Candy Land. *We look like Candy Land,* I thought, *so it would be great if we had a customized game board featuring Village landmarks.*

It would allow wish families to take a bit of the Village with them when their trip ended—a game that would help them remember the special moments they shared as a family. I was sure if I called Hasbro and explained who we were and what we wanted, they would do it. *Why wouldn't they?* I thought.

So I phoned the company's chief of corporate philanthropy, whom I'd met years earlier at a marketing forum, and explained the proposal. Karen Davis was gracious as ever, but the call ended with something along the lines of, "Don't call us; we'll call you."

I understood. The company was already busy with an enormous portfolio of charities. They sent us gifts for our families—which was nice—but not quite what we were hoping for.

I knew if I could sit with Karen and talk face-to-face, she'd see the value in helping. So a few months later, I called again—and, this time, I told a fib.

"Karen, I'm going to be up in your area," I told her. "Can I come by and see you?"

Now this was early December in Rhode Island, and, quite frankly, nobody is just going to "be in the area." But to my surprise, she said, "Yes, stop by and visit."

It was right about then—just after I'd hung up—that I had one of those moments where coincidence looks a lot like magic. Going through my mail, I found a letter from a family who'd written to say they'd had a terrific time at the Village. Their only disappointment? On their last night in town, they stayed too late at the Magic Kingdom and had missed a bedtime tuck-in from Mayor Clayton, the good-natured leader of our Village.

Glancing at the envelope, I saw the family was from Norwood, Massachusetts, and Norwood was only forty minutes from Hasbro's headquarters in Providence. Suddenly, I really did have a reason to "be in the area."

I grabbed the phone and called the mother who'd sent the letter.

"I'm coming to your area," I told her. "How about if I bring Mayor Clayton and we do a tuck-in at your house?"

She was overjoyed!

So Mayor Clayton and I headed north in a December blizzard. The snow and the cold didn't matter; the family had carrot cake waiting for us, and the Mayor tucked the children into bed.

The next morning, we drove to Providence through the still-raging snowstorm to meet Karen and other Hasbro representatives. My son had created a mock-up of the special Candy Land game we'd envisioned, using photos shot by my daughter. After an excellent two-hour meeting, Karen sat back in her chair.

"It's a little busy at a toy company in December, but we love this project," she said. "Give us through the rest of the year, and we'll revisit it in January."

I was thrilled . . . but not quite ready to declare victory.

So, over the next several weeks, I periodically sent Karen copies of some of the email messages and letters we received from wish families. I wanted her to see just how much the Village meant to those kids and their parents. Early in January, I emailed her one of the most poignant notes we'd ever received. Five minutes later, Karen was on the line.

"Stop with the letters," she laughed. "You have your Candy Land game."

It was now January 2006, and our goal was to have a prototype of the game ready for our twentieth anniversary on March 7.

Hasbro knocked it out of the park.

A couple of months later, Karen and her team came to Orlando and presented the company's new version of the board game at our twentieth anniversary celebration. It was a huge hit, and the beginning of a beautiful partnership. But our connection was about to grow even stronger.

When Karen returned to Rhode Island, she had a voicemail waiting for her from a Hasbro employee named Rich:

> *Karen, you don't know me. I work in the finance department here at Hasbro. My son, Matthew, has an inoperable brain tumor, and we just came back from this incredible place called Give Kids The World. I can't believe that Hasbro isn't involved with them.*

Karen immediately called me. We couldn't believe the timing: Karen and this family had literally crossed paths in the air. And just as Rich was imploring Hasbro to support Give Kids The World, the custom Candy Land game was about to go into production.

Karen and I decided to invite Rich's son, Matthew, to the launch of the new game. I'd head back to Rhode Island to be there as the first games rolled off the assembly line, and I'd give the first one to Matthew. By then, Matthew had already lost one eye to the tumor, but he'd be there to share a very special moment.

As the first game came off the line, I knelt down, gave it to Matthew, and asked him if he recognized anything. His face lit up.

"That's where I had ice cream for breakfast! And that's where the dinosaur spit water on me when I played golf!"

This was the power of creating a board game to represent the place where a child had his most healing experience. It was something our wish kids could take back home—or to their hospital beds—to remind them of our castle, and our ice cream parlor, and Marc's Dino Putt. To help them remember the places where they spent a glorious week, laughing and playing like any other child.

While the games were in production, I wandered the factory floor, watching employees work the assembly line. They were performing tasks like taking small pieces and putting them in the box with the rest of the set.

I started talking to some of the workers and was astonished to learn how long some had been there: twenty years, thirty-eight years, forty-seven years. All of them had spent decades on this assembly line. (That is, in itself, a testament to Hasbro as an employer, but I'll get to that in a second.)

I told them a bit about the Village and about the significance of the game pieces they were adding to the box—how these games were for children with critical illnesses, children like Matthew, the son of their Hasbro colleague. After I shared that, I watched as they sat up a bit taller, plucking pieces off the line and fitting them into the game.

They felt connected to this game and their fellow team members. They realized their task had purpose and meaning.

The Hasbro Model

What I didn't fully understand on the day I made that cold call to Hasbro was that the company has a long-standing commitment to social impact. Its commitment to doing good is a model for other companies. Just about any organization could learn a great deal from Hasbro.

The company was founded in 1923 by the Hassenfeld brothers, whose abbreviation, Hasbro, became the official company name in 1968. It was grandson Stephen Hassenfeld and his brother, Alan, who believed deeply in philanthropy and made it a part of the company's culture. Stephen created the Hasbro Children's Fund, and the company would go on to become the major sponsor of the children's hospital in Rhode Island that now bears its name. But the company's dedication to "doing good" goes well beyond corporate donations.

Hasbro was among the first companies to allow employees to use paid time to volunteer. Each employee is allowed to take four hours every month to volunteer with children. Today, 94 percent of Hasbro workers participate in that program. Compare that to the toy-industry average, in which around 40 percent of workers are engaged in some kind of charitable activity with kids.

While many executives would balk at the cost of such an extensive volunteer program, Hasbro is confident that fostering a culture of volunteerism represents a sound business move. Karen Davis, who now has two titles— vice president of community relations and senior vice president of global philanthropy and social impact—has witnessed how volunteerism has helped many employees grow into leadership roles. For some, volunteering is their first exposure to managing people.

"It completely enhances their skill sets," Karen says.

A quick look at the numbers confirms that all this giving back hasn't damaged Hasbro's bottom line. Hasbro is one of the largest toy companies in the world, with net annual revenue of more than $5 billion. Its reputation as a socially responsible company has only boosted its status. When it earned the top ranking on the 2017 Best Corporate Citizens list, it became an even more attractive purchase for the many investors who are seeking socially responsible portfolios.

It has also made Hasbro a sought-after place to work.

"Many new hires are making decisions about which job offer to accept based on the reputation of the company," Karen told *Forbes* magazine.[16] "I've had so many people tell me that they've come to work at Hasbro because of what we do [in social responsibility]."

And once they're on the job at Hasbro, they remain engaged and active—"and engaged means willing to go above and beyond," she told me in an interview. "I think you can make the direct correlation between what we're doing and the bottom line for the company."

And yet Karen is clear that, for Hasbro, and certainly for her personally, boosting profits is not the point of giving back.

"Most of us want to know that, regardless of what we do for a living, at the end of the day, we're doing something that makes a difference," she told *Forbes*. "So it is part of my job to translate to our employees that they are very much a part of this work, and without them, we couldn't make a difference." When it comes to her own job description, she said, "I feel like I've been given something very precious in finding ways to use these resources to help others."[17]

Boundless Impact

We've been enormously fortunate to be on the receiving end of those resources. Hasbro's customized Candy Land game was just the

16   Emily Bennington, "Love the Giving Season? Hasbro VP Tells You How to Make a Career Out of Making a Difference," *Forbes*, November 19, 2012, https://www. forbes.com/sites/emilybennington/2012/11/19/love-the-giving-season-hasbro-vp-tells-you-how-to-make-a-career-out-of-making-a-difference/#d278c8d4e1c6.

17   Ibid.

beginning of our partnership. The company soon became the underwriter of what would be called the Boundless Playground.

When Karen first visited the Village to deliver the Candy Land game, she mentioned the idea of building an inclusive playground: one accessible to all kids, regardless of their limitations. The wish kids who visit the Village come with all different abilities, and their siblings tend to be able-bodied kids, so we need facilities truly designed to accommodate everyone. Karen was excited about the idea of designing and building such a versatile playground.

So we began to draw up a design that was laid out just like the Candy Land game, and the majority of the play area would be wheelchair-accessible.

During construction, Matthew, the son of the Hasbro employee who had been a wish child at the Village, passed away. He was eight years old. With his parents' permission, the facility was named Matthew's Boundless Playground.

Hasbro's commitment to "doing good" and supporting the Village has never been stronger. Teams of Hasbro employees regularly fly to Orlando to visit Give Kids The World and hand out Hasbro toys during our weekly Christmas celebrations.

"They get to see the joy that our products bring those children," Karen explains. "The joy that the families have and the lasting memories of that week are critically important [to the wish child and their families], and we feel privileged to be able to be a part of it."

She said it doesn't matter whether the Hasbro employee is a toy designer or an accountant or an assembly-line worker. Everyone's role is essential to the organization and to bringing joy to wish kids and their families. Hasbro's message to all its team members is clear: "Without you, we can't do the work. Everybody plays a role."

There is a running list of Hasbro employees waiting their turn to visit the Village. And while they wait for their opportunity, *every* Hasbro employee can read letters from wish kids and their families— letters sent to the company every day to thank them for supporting the Village. Letters that make crystal clear the value in being part of the "greater good."

It's all the result of connecting the dots. More than a decade later, the custom board game that Hasbro created for the Village has brought happiness to countless families, who can relive their wish trip together on the living room floor or around a hospital bed. Hasbro, meanwhile, connects the dots between the toys they make, the communities in which they operate, the social causes they serve, and the role of each employee in making it all possible.

Lessons in Connecting the Dots

- Leaders must be able to look across the landscape of current and future trends to connect opportunities that are ripe for leveraging. Alex and Ani saw the way the jewelry market was changing, moving away from anonymous baubles and toward accessories that carry a particular purpose. They married that trend with charitable goals to create a formula for exponential growth—measured in both profit and impact.

- Organizations must connect the dots for customers, employees, and partners to tell a bigger story that fosters engagement. Hasbro makes philanthropy a part of its business model and helps its employees understand that *their* contribution is what allows the company to make a real difference.

- At Give Kids The World, a partnership with Hasbro allowed us to create a custom board game—something that might seem like just a set of plastic pieces and some colorful cardboard. But over the past decade, the game has brought happiness to too many families to count. It was all because we connected the dots between families' wish-trip experiences at the Village and how we could continue to help them back at home.

PART FOUR:

CHAMPION POSSIBILITY

The best companies make it personal, forge powerful partnerships, connect the dots, and champion possibility. At organizations that champion possibility, leaders remain open to exploring new ideas—especially those from their front-line workers—and continually solicit feedback from stakeholders to create a culture of innovation. They recognize that the best ideas may come from the bottom up, and they encourage staff members to bring them forward.

In this chapter, I'll explain how we've championed possibility at the Village, and how the ideas and feedback from key players both inside and outside our organization have shaped Give Kids The World for the better.

These are strategies that organizations large and small, for profit and not, can use to energize their culture, brainstorm new and better products, and boost engagement for the long term.

Cookies and Conversations

Start with the basics. Soliciting honest feedback from staff can be tricky, especially in large organizations where employees on the front line may be intimidated by the idea of telling management what they really think. That's why it's crucial to start at the most human level by creating comfortable spaces where employees and leaders can get together to talk. That's why I created a tradition called "Cookies and Conversations."

It's pretty much what it sounds like.

Twice a year, I invite all our staff to come up to spend a couple of hours munching on cookies and chatting with one another—and with me. It's important that everyone on our team, no matter where they sit, has the chance to make themselves heard. I believe that on principle, but I also know it's a smart strategy.

I need *their* feedback in order to do *my* job. To say that I can't fulfill my responsibilities without them is an enormous understatement, as they're the ones making our vision come alive day in and day out. When something's amiss, they know about it. I've got to keep the lines of communication open so that my team can pass vital information on to me or to other members of the leadership team. And while that might sound like common sense, the truth is that it's anything but common practice at many companies.

Prior to starting Cookies and Conversations, when our staff was much smaller, I made a point of meeting every staff member once a year in December. I'd spend fifteen minutes or so with each person, time they could use to talk about anything they wanted—the organization, their role, or even their family. The idea was that they had time to express anything they wanted to share with me.

Now that we've grown exponentially—to a staff of 180—I can't meet individually with everyone on our team, so I do Cookies and Conversations with every department. The night before those meetings, I bake all the cookies and brownies. It's important to me that everything is homemade. Then I invite each department and ask the team members what's on their mind. I encourage them to ask me questions. This gives me the chance to hear what's being talked about around the Village. If they've heard a rumor, I urge them to bring it up. Rather than let any potential problem fester, I prefer to address it openly. I also request that supervisors attend different sessions from their employees, so that everyone can be completely honest.

Of course, the title "president" or "CEO" intimidates some people, and the first few minutes of each Cookies and Conversations can be awkward. Like patients in a doctor's waiting room, folks sit quietly, waiting for someone to break the ice. It's my job to ease that tension and make myself approachable, and I've found that people relax if I kick off the meeting with an update about what's happening at the Village—anything to get the group chatting.

I know that the concept of Cookies and Conversations isn't earth shattering or entirely unique. Other companies put their own spin on the idea. Walt Disney World Resort, for example, holds "You've got to be kidding me" sessions, which invite cast members to identify some frustrating parts of their jobs.

In the early days, Disney wasn't always so tuned in to its employees. After the opening of the Walt Disney World Resort, executives were so focused on the guest experience that they overlooked cast members. Backstage areas were neglected and turnover was high. The first cast opinion poll was a wake-up call. Leaders quickly embraced the concept that if you take care of your people, they will take care of your guests, and the business results will follow.

Executive Vice President of Operations Lee Cockerell knew that leadership excellence was at the core of this formula, so he launched an ambitious personal research project to determine, in part, the expectations of cast members and guests.

Lee went person to person, conducting hundreds of interviews. Gradually, as the information piled up, Lee reached a startling conclusion: the priorities and needs of guests and cast members were almost identical. Both groups wanted the following:

- To feel special

- To be treated as individuals

- To be respected

On a fourth item, they differed only slightly. Guests wanted access to knowledgeable cast members who could answer their questions. Cast members wanted access to the training and tools needed to provide the right information and do their jobs well.

Lee described his findings in the book "Creating Magic," and when he first shared them with me, I was struck by how simple and powerful they were. They reinforced the belief that if you take care of your people, your people will take care of your guests.

I've been guided by that philosophy ever since, and it's why I feel it's crucial to create opportunities for top leaders to mingle with frontline employees. You have no idea when someone in your company is holding a key insight. They may not even realize it's a key insight. And, either way, they're certainly not going to take the elevator up to the C-suite to tell you about it.

It's your job—and my job—to create the environment and the opportunities for people to share their perspective and their unique expertise. I've heard too many corporate managers say, after learning about a smoldering fire, "Why didn't they *tell* me that?"

The answer is simple: the manager never asked.

Cookies and Conversations is one (delicious) way for me to ask. It helps us identify problems and create solutions. And it lets employees shape the future of this organization, ultimately strengthening their connection to it.

Here's one example of how this organization has been shaped for the better by insights that came from a conversation over cookies.

Historically, Give Kids The World had rejected the idea of having an on-site souvenir shop. This was for a very particular reason that, we felt, was rooted in who we are: the wish trip is a free vacation for our families. At home, their lives are stressful; day in, day out, they are battling their child's illness. Their wish trip is supposed to be a worry-free vacation, and, we believed, that meant there should be no monetary transactions. They pay nothing when they want ice cream. There's no transaction when they eat dinner. Our staff and volunteers will not accept tips. It is simply not a practice to exchange money between families and Give Kids The World.

But a day hardly went by without a guest asking where they could buy a Village-themed T-shirt or souvenir, or a postcard to send to someone back home. The way we handled those requests was to assist guests in using our online gift shop. Our volunteers provided guests with the online order forms and a code for free shipping. Then the guests filled out the form and we mailed them their souvenirs. Meanwhile, the merchandise they were purchasing was sitting in our warehouse, a mere three hundred feet away.

It was at a Cookies and Conversations session that a front-desk staffer raised the issue. I give her a great deal of credit for voicing the matter directly to me; it was a clear sign that Cookies and Conversations was achieving its purpose.

"We're here to say 'yes' to our families," she said to me, as her peers listened. "And when they ask to buy a souvenir, we're basically telling them 'no.' We're saying they have to go home to their busy lives and *then* we'll accept their money, but not while they're here and it's easy."

It was a darn good point. I told her that I would take her suggestion to the leadership team.

When I did, there was resistance. Some of our top managers did not want to introduce any form of financial transaction into the Village. But what prevailed was an agreement to pilot the proposal in a minimalist format: We would start with just a shelf of souvenirs behind the front desk, and we would do that immediately. Then we would evaluate how it was going. If we didn't feel like it was working out, we would can it. (This is a crucial aspect of championing possibility at any organization: it's OK if an idea doesn't work! When one thing bombs, just try something else. Keep at it until you hit the right formula.)

Well, it worked. Families loved it. The shelf behind the front desk soon expanded to a dedicated area in the House of Hearts, our guest-services building. Within a year or two, it grew again, into an actual gift shop. And a couple years after that, it grew yet again, into the Memory Market. It's a space that isn't just about buying souvenirs. At the Memory Market, guests can check out devices to capture photos and videos from their wish trip, and then our staff will upload all of their digital memories to the cloud for them to enjoy back home.

The gift shop has been a huge hit and a win all around. We improved the experience for our guests and for our employees. We also fulfilled a need for our visiting volunteers, who want to purchase items to commemorate their volunteer experience.

On top of all that, we improved our bottom line. The Memory Market has become a valuable revenue stream, bringing in more than $500,000 a year. And it was all thanks to some homemade cookies and casual conversation.

The Employee-Satisfaction Survey

At the Village, we're not afraid to acknowledge to our employees that this place isn't perfect—that *they* are essential in helping us improve both their experience and the experience of all our stakeholders. We're always developing and growing, and we want to know what they need from us in order to do their jobs even better. Cookies and Conversations is one important way of soliciting input from staff. But some types of feedback require anonymity.

For over a decade, we've conducted an annual employee-satisfaction survey. We underscore to all staff the importance of the survey—assuring them all responses are anonymous—and urge everyone to participate. That's pretty easy for administrative staff, who are at their computers all day. But for engineers, housekeepers, entertainment coordinators, and food-and-beverage folks, it can be difficult to take time out of the day. They hit the ground running the moment they punch in. So we make the survey a priority. To give those frontline workers a chance to fill out the questionnaire, managers step in and take over their job duties.

It's worth it. That employee survey has shed light on a host of issues, large and small, and helped us find smart ways to make things even better. Recent feedback, for example, revealed significant interest in a tuition-reimbursement program, a benefit that's uncommon in nonprofit organizations. We took that suggestion to our leadership team. Within a year, we unveiled a new tuition program.

This innovation is already helping great people move up in the ranks. It prompted one of our part-time employees to come on as a full-timer. Thanks to the tuition assistance, she's now pursuing her degree with an eye toward advancing still further at the Village.

Another great idea to come from the employee surveys? English classes for our housekeeping staff.

We had offered such classes in the past, but attendance was spotty. The survey helped us determine why. Turns out, our original English class wasn't especially effective because it tried to accommodate students of all levels of fluency. Housekeepers just learning English were in the same class as those with much more experience. The mix of abilities was counterproductive.

Armed with that information, we implemented a new program that divides students by fluency. It was a huge win for our housekeepers, and a huge step forward for us in retaining these crucial staff members.

"I'm watching them interview for jobs now," said Caroline Schumacher, our VP of operations, about our housekeepers who have gone through English classes. "They're looking at jobs outside of housekeeping. They're applying in reservations and other departments. When we can mix our bilingual staff around and get them in more guest-facing positions, it's a win all around."

The survey also helps us gauge how we're doing on the crucial metric of employee engagement. In our 2017 survey, 84 percent of respondents agreed with the statement, "I plan to continue my career with this organization for at least two more years." Meanwhile, a whopping 99 percent of respondents in 2017 agreed with the statement, "I understand the importance of my role to the success of the organization."

The Villas Don't Have Carpets: What It Means to Truly Listen

It's particularly important—and useful—to solicit input from frontline team members before launching any major new undertaking. Doing so engenders staff buy-in and helps prevent problems instead of having to correct them later.

A few years ago, we were planning a major expansion: adding twenty-four villas to our existing 144 units. This growth would allow us to accommodate an additional 1,300 wish families every year—a huge leap forward in our capacity to fulfill our mission. But the internal planning was complex to say the least.

We started this enormous project in a way that might surprise you: some of our earliest meetings were with our housekeeping staff. We did that because we wanted their feedback. After all, these are the folks who are in the villas every day. They know what works and what doesn't, and we wanted to ask them, "How can we make the units easier to keep clean?"

The answer, it turned out, was simple.

No carpet.

Carpet, they pointed out, is where dirt and stains go to hide. They could vacuum three times a day, but the carpet would never be completely clean. Design villas with hard floors, they said. Cleaning hard floors would be easier and would allow them to devote more time to keeping the rest of the villas spotless.

So that's what we did, and it has worked out beautifully.

Organizations of every size and shape and tax status pour loads of money into trying to find out what customers want. That's important, of course, but they should be equally committed to figuring out what employees want. If businesses devoted more energy to addressing employees' wants and needs by truly championing possibility, they would ultimately have a much easier time delivering value to customers. They would also build an enviable internal culture along the way.

Reimagining Customer Service

Cookies and Conversations and the employee-satisfaction survey had been fixtures at the Village for a number of years when we decided to try a still bolder process for soliciting new and even off-the-wall ideas: we undertook a years-long process of rebuilding our guest services from the ground up.

Through customer surveys and staff feedback, we'd come to realize that some aspects of our check-in and orientation didn't make sense for our wish families. The process—for us—moved smoothly enough, but it overwhelmed some families. After traveling all day, they just wanted to get to their villas, not sit through a sixty-minute orientation.

We knew we needed to focus relentlessly on what works best for our guests. We wanted to look at every detail through *their* eyes. It was time to completely reimagine the way we delivered guest services.

To make over our process, we enlisted help from an Orlando design consultant who made an incredible commitment to the Village: Chad Hostetler took a six-month sabbatical from his collaborative design company, White Oaks Design, to do a full-time volunteer stint as our director of excellence and innovation. He led the effort to revamp guest services.

We asked twenty-five employees and volunteers to join the brainstorm and think about how we could improve. We had folks from engineering and development and housekeeping and warehousing all in one room. "Come up with new ways of serving our guests," we said. *Nothing* was off the table.

"The design sessions were about really putting everyone in the shoes of the guests," Chad recalls. "We took an average-sized family of five and created big cardboard cutouts of each family member. And then we said, 'OK. As a newborn, here are my needs and wants. As a toddler, here are my needs and wants. As a twelve- to fifteen-year-old, here are my needs, interests, and wants. As a mother, here are my needs, interests, and wants.' You've got to put yourself into those shoes."

Meanwhile, when we said that nothing was off the table, we meant it. To encourage more creativity and playfulness, we imagined what guest services would look like at the Crayola Hotel. What would the lobby look like if this were the Apple Village? Or Nike Village? Or the Pixar Hotel?

"It was a process of unlocking our brains," Chad says.

This newfound sense of imagination permeated the Village, as staff and volunteers looked for ways to make our guest experience even better. All told, those brainstorming sessions generated about two hundred new ideas.

The original mission—reimagining guest services—produced dramatic results. We began calling families a week before their arrival to help them plan their itineraries. We initiated curbside check-in, so families could get into their villas more quickly. Orientation is now done in a family's villa, not a Village meeting room. We improved internal communications, so we could quickly have a villa ready for a family that arrived before the standard 3 p.m. check-in. We sought to personalize the process as much as possible.

The project sparked changes across departments. Like Disney, where cast members are empowered to go the extra mile for guests, we moved toward a culture that encourages everyone to make decisions in the moment to take care of our families in any way they see fit. As long as they're abiding by basic safety rules, staff and volunteers don't have to go up the chain of command for approval.

That's led to some pretty inventive acts of service. In one case, an employee enlisted the help of the local sanitation department, so a wish child could get a ride in a garbage truck. The reason? The kid just loved garbage trucks.

Reimagining guest services was a complicated process, but it produced a simple message that we try to live by every day: if you're improving the experience for our visiting families, just do it.

That's a principle I absorbed early on in my time at Disney. The company was built on the idea of doing everything possible to make guests happy. When I worked there, we learned that "guests may not always be right, but they will always be our guests."

That mindset permeates the organization because it starts at the top. As Walt Disney World Resort President George A. Kalogridis told me, "Our leadership displays the values we want our cast members to exhibit."

All seventy-four thousand Walt Disney World cast members—especially those in guest-facing jobs—are encouraged and authorized to do what's necessary to make a guest feel special. That can be as simple as walking them to an attraction or as spectacular as arranging for a special dinner.

Cadence's story is a perfect example of how Disney's personal approach can touch a family.

Cadence was born with a defective heart. Her family came from Virginia, where her dad was in the military. Cadence was one of eight siblings. And though just three years old, she didn't have much time left.

Cadence's wish was to meet Minnie Mouse. She loved Minnie and wanted more than anything to visit her at Walt Disney World. So arrangements were quickly made to bring her to the Village.

When Cadence arrived, she and her family were whisked off to the Magic Kingdom. The little girl could barely contain herself. She giggled at the characters, marveled at the rides, and discovered a new favorite snack: churros. For this sweet, giddy three-year-old, touring the Magic Kingdom while munching on a churro was the definition of "bliss."

And there was more to come.

As the 3 p.m. parade approached, Cadence's parents looked for a good spot to view the parade. While the family jockeyed for a space, a Disney cast member spotted the family's Give Kids The World buttons. Immediately, he escorted them to coveted front-row seats.

"These seats are perfect," he told the little girl. "You'll have an awesome view."

And so it was that when Minnie rolled by, there was Cadence, in the front row, nibbling a churro and beaming at her favorite character in the world. Minnie turned toward Cadence and waved. Her wish was complete.

Just four hours later, Cadence passed away.

The next day, her grieving parents asked to go back to the Magic Kingdom. They were so grateful to that Disney cast member—so touched by his act of kindness—that they wanted to meet him and tell him how he had fulfilled their daughter's wish.

Because he had taken the initiative—and because he'd been

empowered to do so—he had made Cadence's final hours some of her happiest ever.

It's a simple but powerful principle we try to live by every day: if you're improving the experience for our visiting families, if you've found a way to make their time at the Village even happier, just do it.

Champion the Possibilities

- Solicit honest feedback from staff. Since frontline employees may be intimidated by the idea of telling management what they really think, start at a personal level: create comfortable spaces where employees and leaders can gather together in a relaxed atmosphere with no agenda other than to chat. Provide tasty snacks, too.

- "You've got to be kidding me" sessions are a chance for staff to be completely honest about the aspects of their job that are frustrating. To pull this off, you need two key elements: employees must know they can voice concerns without receiving blowback, and, once identified, issues must receive genuine consideration from management.

- Some types of feedback require anonymity. In addition to open conversations between staff and leadership, use an anonymous survey tool to collect employee feedback on a regular basis. Make sure that employees from all areas of the organization—including, and especially, those who do not typically spend time at a computer—have dedicated paid time during which they can complete the survey.

- When embarking on major new projects, *start* by asking frontline employees for their input.

- When employees know that their ideas will be seriously considered for implementation, you're on your way to creating a culture of innovation. For strategic-planning initiatives, bring together a team drawn from throughout the organization and open up a brainstorming session in which *nothing* is off the table.

PART FIVE:

GIVE, SERVE, SHARE

As I sat down to put the finishing touches on this book, *Forbes* magazine announced that a "tectonic" shift currently underway in the corporate world is the "hunger amongst employees to work for companies that have a higher purpose."[18] The desire to make a positive social or environmental impact now ranks, on average, as workers' number-two career goal, right after making a significant

---

18   Afdhel Aziz, "How Benevity Is Unleashing Employee Purpose as a Competitive Advantage," *Forbes*, July 2, 2018, https://www.forbes.com/sites/afdhelaziz/2018/07/02/how-benevity-is-unleashing-employee-purpose-as-a-competitive-advantage/#799519074c2f.

contribution to their company.

A new generation of organizations has sprung up to help companies understand and adapt to this change. The technology company Goodera, which offers a platform that links for-profit entities with nonprofits around the world, has been providing leadership to HR executives to help them grasp how the millennial workforce differs from Gen X: millennials are demanding workplaces that operate for a social purpose in addition to a profit motive. According to Abhishek Humbad, Goodera's founder, millennials "follow a religion called humanity … They believe in credibility, and credibility comes from how they contribute to the society." Goodera has assisted an army of corporations in understanding that this new crop of workers wants opportunities for volunteerism embedded in their job responsibilities. They want to be able to see the immediate results and impact of their efforts in terms of contributing to a greater good.[19]

And even as employers struggle to adapt to the demands of millennials, Generation Z is coming up behind them. The oldest members of Gen Z were born in the mid-nineties, which means they're now entering the workforce en masse. One study conducted by the Lovell Corporation, which specializes in marketing to young people, found that Gen Z is even *more* committed to the notion of finding purpose-driven work than millennials are.[20] In other words, it appears that this trend isn't going to change anytime soon.

And that's just one of the major shifts rattling the corporate

19   Nikita Shetty, "Attracting, Engaging and Retaining Millennials at the Workplace," *People Matters*, July 18, 2018, https://www.peoplematters.in/article/employee-engagement/attracting-engaging-and-retaining-millennials-at-the-workplace-18797.

20   "The Change Generation Report: How Millennials and Generation Z Are Redefining Work," The Lovell Corporation, 2017, https://www.lovellcorporation.com/wp-content/uploads/2017/11/The2017ChangeGenerationReport-Lovell.pdf.

world, and the world in general. Businesses large and small are struggling to adapt to a competitive environment in which they must be ever more responsive and customized to consumers. Lyft and Uber have upended the transportation industry, while Airbnb has disrupted the hospitality sector worldwide.

Amazon has all but completed its transformation of the world of commerce. Amazon Prime now boasts over one hundred million members worldwide, and Prime membership carries a host of personalized benefits: exclusive services and customized deals for each of those hundred-million-plus members. Prime's dominance prompted *Forbes* to declare that the digital disruption of 2018 was "the consumer preference for personalized products and experiences"—and to note that the traditional consumer packaged goods sector isn't keeping up with the trend.[21]

Chaos in the business world mirrors the upheaval taking place across the nation and around the world.

Politically, we've never been more divided or unsure of what happens next. There seems to be a new humanitarian crisis every week, and the specter of terrorism has become a fixture of our landscape. Even the climate seems to have it in for us, with sea levels rising and wildfires posing ever-greater threats to the American West. Thanks to social media and twenty-four-hour newsfeeds, we have front-row seats to all the bad news.

Our current state of affairs breeds anxiety and, more to the point, threatens to suffocate hope.

No package from Amazon Prime—regardless of how quickly it's delivered—can meet the innate need for hope and purpose in life

---

21 Deborah Weinswig, "What Do Amazon, Nike and Your Favorite Startup Have In Common? Pop-Up Stores," *Forbes*, July 24, 2018, https://www.forbes.com/sites/deborahweinswig/2018/07/24/what-do-amazon-nike-and-your-favorite-startup-have-in-common-pop-up-stores/#73e23b666e17.

that each of us feels. No amount of digital connectivity or product customization can satisfy the desire humans have to make a positive contribution through their life's work.

More companies are recognizing that fact, and a cottage industry has developed around helping corporations identify and articulate their deeper meaning. The central message of this gospel of purpose?

In an age of endless customized options, it's treacherous to compete only on the basis of convenience or price. Instead, build a culture of service and purpose because customers have demonstrated that, products and services being relatively equal, they want to support businesses that embrace social causes. They'll even pay more for it.

Give, Serve, Share

Happily, *every* organization—regardless of size or tax status—can infuse its brand with a sense of purpose by teaming up with the right charitable partner. At the Village, we believe there are three ways to do that. Your company can *give*, it can *serve*, and it can *share*.

That may seem fairly intuitive, but it took some work before we were able to put the idea into words. People were always asking how they could help—fittingly, the same question Henri Landwirth asked when he founded the Village—so, some time ago, we decided to seriously look at that question.

When all was said and done—when we distilled the issue to its essence—we determined that there were really three ways people could help: They could "give"—money or in-kind donations. They could "serve"—volunteer with us. Or they could "share"—spread our story and mission as widely as possible. Hence, give, serve, share.

Though it's been unspoken, that model has guided us for

decades, and it animates many of the partnerships I've highlighted in previous chapters.

Mears Transportation, which I told you about in Part One, gave us a remarkable gift when Henri first created the Village. And for three generations, Mears has felt a sense of mission and meaning as a result of providing transportation for wish families. Likewise for Hasbro—makers of our customized Candy Land game—and Alex and Ani, a company that's seen profits soar as it has supported a range of causes, from clean water to critically ill kids.

In Part Two, I told you about Wyndham, and the improbable undertaking known as Extreme Village Makeover. I introduced you to Brad Loewen who, after the passing of his son, moved his family from Canada to Orlando so family members could devote their lives to volunteering at the Village.

Each of those relationships—and many more—embody, in some way, the notion of *give, serve, share.* They are invaluable to the Village—in fact, we couldn't survive without them—but they also benefit our partners by providing the deeper purpose and meaning companies increasingly seek.

That search for meaning—the desire to make a difference—is a powerful motivator, and it has landed me in some pretty unusual situations. In the name of charity, I've raced snowmobiles in temperatures so frigid I thought my lungs might crack. I've shot skeet while standing in a port-o-let in the bayou, and I've kissed a full-grown boar square on the snout.

In some cases, the need to be part of something bigger than oneself can bring an entire community together. Which brings me to the Mickey Maniacs.

The Maniacs' story begins in 2001, after a phys-ed teacher from Cut Off, Louisiana, discovered the Village while vacationing in

Central Florida. That teacher, a woman named Michelle Plaisance, was so moved by our mission that when she returned home, she made a presentation about Give Kids The World at a schoolwide assembly. Her message struck a chord, in part because several children from the community had been wish children at the Village.

So, Michelle and her students dubbed themselves the "Mickey Maniacs"—Michelle is a *huge* Disney fan—and began hosting events to spread the word about Give Kids The World. They organized bake sales, car washes, golf tournaments, even swim-a-thons. Then, they took their initiative a step further.

Michelle began bringing students to the Village's annual 5K fundraiser. Before making the seven-hundred-mile trip, they'd spend weeks raising money and telling everyone they met about Give Kids The World.

In the nineteen years since Michelle made her first presentation about Give Kids The World, Larose–Cut Off Middle School families have done something astonishing. This single middle school from small-town Louisiana has raised more than $900,000 for the Village. Their commitment and success are staggering.

So, what makes the Maniacs or Brad Loewen's company or an international corporation like Hasbro special when it comes to embracing meaningful causes? Are they unique or different?

Not really—at least not in any way that matters.

The only thing that sets these groups and businesses apart from the herd is their conscious decision to foster a sense of purpose and support causes that move them. And the great news is, any organization can do the same, regardless of size. Whether you have a team of twelve, twelve thousand, or one hundred thousand, there are opportunities everywhere to align with charitable causes, boost employee engagement, contribute to the greater good, and improve your bottom line.

We live in complicated, messy, anxious times. It's tempting, some days, to want to crawl under a blanket and shut it all out. But don't.

Instead, search for places like the Village—places or causes that are filled with hope. The Village radiates light even on the darkest days. People come to give, serve, and share—and, in that, they find meaning and purpose.

A volunteer I know described it to me this way:

He said he'd spent years working, building a career, and raising a family. He was generally happy—parts of his life were fabulous— but often he felt like he was treading water. He expected more, not wealth or possessions, but a sense that what he did really mattered.

He began volunteering at the Village and was soon struck by what he saw in his fellow volunteers.

"I felt like I was surrounded by people who'd discovered the secret to happiness," he said. "And pretty soon, I felt like that, too."

He discovered what so many of us spend so long searching for: Happiness comes from committing to a cause that's bigger than yourself. Happiness comes from purpose.

From here at Give Kids The World, I urge you and your team to find that purpose. Get involved with the Village or any other organization that moves you. Your life will never be the same.

ABOUT GIVE KIDS THE WORLD VILLAGE

Give Kids The World Village is an 84-acre, nonprofit resort in Central Florida that provides weeklong, cost-free vacations to children with critical illnesses and their families.

The Village and its community partners provide children and their families accommodations in fully-furnished villas, transportation, tickets to theme parks, meals, daily entertainment and much more.

Each year 27,000 children in the United States are diagnosed with a critical illness. Half of all children eligible for a wish through a partnering wish-granting organization choose to visit Central Florida and its collection of world-famous theme parks and other attractions.

Our goal, quite simply, is to provide everything these families need to make their trip the vacation of a lifetime. Since 1986, more than 165,000 children and families have had their dreams fulfilled in a whimsical Village unlike any other place on earth.

Charity Navigator has named Give Kids The World Village a Four-Star Charity – the highest ranking possible – 13 years in a row. For more information, visit www.gktw.org.

ABOUT THE AUTHOR,
PAMELA LANDWIRTH

Pamela Landwirth has been part of Give Kids The World since 1992, and was chosen to lead the Village in 1995. As President and CEO, she is responsible for the operations of the Village and all strategic advancement initiatives for the organization.

Prior to joining the Village, Pamela developed an extensive background in resort operations management, human resource development, and project planning from her 16 years with the Walt Disney World Company.

Under Pamela's leadership, virtually every aspect of Give Kids The World Village has been transformed. The Village more than doubled in size, 11 new venues and attractions have been added, and volunteer shifts have quadrupled.

But most importantly, the number of families who visit Give Kids The World Village each year has grown from 3,949 in 1995 to almost 8,000 today. Pamela's dedication to those families is tireless, and she works each day to create for them the happiness that inspires hope.

In addition to her work at the Village, Pamela is a highly sought-after speaker and has served on several nonprofit boards. She has a bachelor's degree in History from the University of Georgia and a master's degree in Business Administration from Rollins College. Pamela lives outside Orlando and has three grown children.

pamelalandwirth.com

CPSIA information can be obtained
at www.ICGtesting.com
Printed in the USA
FFHW012008060519
52329005-57682FF